Poems by a Slave

Poetry Written by an African American in Chapel Hill, North Carolina during the 1820s and 1830s

By George Moses Horton

PANTIANOS
CLASSICS

Published by Pantianos Classics

ISBN-13: 978-1-78987-477-8

First published in 1837

Photograph of a commemorative plaque in North Carolina

Contents

Explanation.. *vi*

Preface to the Second Edition.................................... *ix*

Praise of Creation 11

On The Silence of A Young Lady............................... 14

The Lover's Farewell.. 16

On Liberty and Slavery.. 18

To Eliza... 20

Love 21

On The Death of an Infant... 22

The Slave's Complaint 23

On The Truth of the Saviour 25

On Spring.. 27

On Summer.. 29

On Winter.. 32

Heavenly Love... 34

On The Death of Rebecca.. 36

On Death.. 38

On The Evening and Morning................................... 40

On The Poetic Muse 42

Consequences of Happy Marriages.......................... 44

Lines 46

To The Gad-Fly.. 49

The Loss of Female Character 51

Explanation

GEORGE, who is the author of the following poetical effusions, is a Slave, the property of Mr. James Horton, of Chatham County, North Carolina. He has been in the habit, some years past, of producing poetical pieces, sometimes on suggested subjects, to such persons as would write them while he dictated. Several compositions of his have already appeared in the Raleigh Register. Some have made their way into the Boston newspapers, and have evoked expressions of approbation and surprise. Many persons have now become much interested in the promotion of his prospects, some of whom are elevated in office and literary attainments. They are solicitous that efforts at length be made to obtain by subscription, a sum sufficient for his emancipation, upon the condition of his going in the vessel which shall first afterwards sail for Liberia. It is his earnest and only wish to become a member of that Colony, to enjoy its privileges, and apply his industry and mental abilities, to the promotion of its prospects and his own. It is upon these terms alone, that the efforts of those who befriend his views are intended to have a final effect.

To put to trial the plan here urged in his behalf, the paper now exhibited is published, Several of his productions are contained in the succeeding pages. Many more might have been added, which would have swelled into a larger size. They would doubtless be interesting to many, but it is hoped that the specimens here inserted will be sufficient to accomplish the object of the publication. Expense will thus be avoided, and the money better employed in enlarging the sum applicable for his emancipation. - It is proposed, that in every town or vicinity where contributions are made, they may be put into the hands of some person, who will humanely consent to receive them, and give notice to Mr. *Weston R. Gales,* in Raleigh, of the amount collected. As soon as it is ascertained that the collections will accomplish the object, it is expected that they will be transmitted without delay to Mr. *Weston R. Gales,* But should they ultimately prove insufficient, they will be returned to subscribers.

None will imagine it possible that pieces produced as these have been, should be free from blemish in composition or taste. The author is now 32 years of age, and has always laboured in the field on his master's farm, promiscuously with the few others which Mr. Horton owns, in circumstances of the greatest possible simplicity. His master says he knew nothing of his poetry, but as he heard of it from others. George knows how to read, and is now learning to write. All his pieces are written down by others; and his reading, which is done at night, and at the usual intervals allowed to slaves, has been much employed on poetry, such as he could procure, this being the species of composition most interesting to him. It is thought best to print his productions without correction, that the mind of the reader may be in no uncertainty as to the originality and genuineness of every part. We shall conclude this account of George, with an assurance that he has been ever a faithful, honest and industrious slave. That his heart has felt deeply and sensitively in this lowest possible condition of human nature, will easily be believed, and is impressively confirmed by one of his stanzas,

> Come, melting Pity, from afar,
> And break this vast enormous oar
>   Between a wretch and thee;
> Purchase a few short days of time,
> And bid a vassal soar sublime,
>   On wings of Liberty.

Raleigh, July 2, 1829.

Preface to the Second Edition

Of these poems, the present publisher has never seen or heard of but one copy, which was recently obtained by Joshua Coffin, of this city, from a gentleman who met with it in Cincinnati a few years ago. The pamphlet is republished, without any alterations, - even verbal; except the insertion of the headline, "Poems by a slave," over the pages, and the omission of the title page, which ran as follows:

"The Hope of Liberty, containing a number of poetical pieces. By George M. Horton. Raleigh, printed by Gales & Son, 1829."

Observe 1st, That Gales, the printer of the pamphlet, is now one of the firm of Gales & Seaton, at Washington, - *no abolitionist.* 2nd, The publisher admits slavery to be "the lowest possible condition of human nature;" and that the slaves are not all happy, for George "felt deeply and sensitively." 3d, The man who could write such poems was kept for 32 years in "the lowest possible condition of human nature," and was to remain there if he would not consent to go to Liberia.

Whether the poems sold for sufficient to buy this man, so dangerous to "Southern institutions," and export him, I have not been able to ascertain. Perhaps George is still a slave!

L. C, G.

Philadelphia, September, 1837.

=====

Immediately after the present edition was issued, the following letter was put into my hands.   Publisher.

Washington, September 12*th,* 1837.

Dear Sir: - I have inquired of Mr. Gales, agreeably to your request to 'ascertain the present condition of *George M. Norton*. He informs me that he is still the slave of James Horton of Chatham County, and is employed as a servant at Chapel Hill, the seat of the University of North Carolina. It is understood by Mr. G. that he did not derive much pecuniary profit from the publication of his poems; and that, since the death of his patron, the late Dr. Caldwell, President of the University he has attended to other occupations.

I am,

Yours truly,

Mr. Joshua Coffin.   * * * *

Praise of Creation

Creation fires my tongue!
  Nature thy anthems raise;
And spread the universal song
  Of thy Creator's praise!

Heaven's chief delight was Man
  Before Creation's birth -
Ordained with joy to lead the van,
  And reign the lord of earth.

When Sin was quite unknown,
  And all the woes it brought,
He hailed the morn without a groan
  Or one corroding thought.

When each revolving wheel
  Assumed its sphere sublime,
Submissive Earth then heard the peal,
  And struck the march of time.

The march in Heaven begun,
  And splendor filled the skies,
When Wisdom bade the morning Sun
  With joy from chaos rise.

The angels heard the tune
 Throughout creation ring;
They seized their golden harps as soon
 And touched on every string.

When time and space were young,
 And music rolled along -
The morning stars together sung,
 And Heaven was drown'd in song.

Ye towering eagles soar,
 And fan Creation's blaze,
And ye terrific lions roar,
 To your Creator's praise.

Responsive thunders roll,
 Loud acclamations sound,
And show your Maker's vast control
 O'er all the worlds around.

Stupendous mountains smoke,
 And lift your summits high,
To him who all your terrors woke,
 Dark'ning the sapphire sky.

Now let my muse descend,
 To view the march below -
Ye subterraneous worlds attend
 And bid your chorus flow.

Ye vast volcanoes yell
    Whence fiery cliffs are hurled;
And all ye liquid oceans swell
    Beneath the solid world.

Ye cataracts combine,
    Nor let the paean cease -
The universal concert join,
    Thou dismal precipice.

But halt my feeble tongue,
    My weary muse delays:
But, oh my soul, still float along
    Upon the flood of praise!

On The Silence of A Young Lady

On account of the imaginary flight of her suitor

Oh, heartless dove! mount in the skies,
  Spread thy soft wing upon the gale,
Or on thy sacred pinions rise,
  Nor brood with silence in the vale.

Breathe on the air thy plaintive note,
  Which oft has filled the lonesome grove,
And let thy melting ditty float -
  The dirge of long lamented love.

Coo softly to the silent ear,
  And make the floods of grief to roll;
And cause by love the sleeping tear,
  To wake with sorrow from the soul.

Is it the loss of pleasures past
  Which makes thee droop thy sounding wing?
Does winter's rough, inclement blast
  Forbid thy tragic voice to sing?

Is it because the fragrant breeze
  Along the sky forbears to flow -
Nor whispers low amidst the trees,

Whilst all the vallies frown below?
Why should a frown thy soul alarm,
    And tear thy pleasures from thy breast?
Or veil the smiles of every charm,
    And rob thee of thy peaceful rest.

Perhaps thy sleeping love may wake,
    And hear thy penitential tone;
And suffer not thy heart to break,
    Nor let a princess grieve alone.

Perhaps his pity may return,
    With equal feeling from the heart,
And breast with breast together burn,
    Never - no, never more to part.

Never, till death's resistless blow,
    Whose call the dearest must obey -
In twain together then may go,
    And thus together dwell for aye.

Say to the suitor, Come away,
    Nor break the knot which love has tied -
Nor to the world thy trust betray,
    And fly for ever from thy bride.

The Lover's Farewell

And wilt thou, love, my soul display,
And all my secret thoughts betray?
I strove, but could not hold thee fast,
My heart flies off with thee at last.

The favorite daughter of the dawn,
On love's mild breeze will soon be gone;
I strove, but could not cease to love,
Nor from my heart the weight remove.

And wilt thou, love, my soul beguile,
And gull thy fav'rite with a smile?
Nay, soft affection answers, nay,
And beauty wings my heart away.

I steal on tiptoe from these bowers,
All spangled with a thousand flowers;
I sigh, yet leave them all behind,
To gain the object of my mind.

And wilt thou, love, command my soul,
And waft me with a light control? -
Adieu to all the blooms of May,
Farewell - I fly with love away!

I leave my parents here behind,
And all my friends to love resigned -
'Tis grief to go, but death to stay:
Farewell - I'm. gone with love away!

On Liberty and Slavery

Alas! and am I born for this,
  To wear this slavish chain?
Deprived of all created bliss,
  Through hardship, toil and pain!

How long have I in bondage lain,
  And languished to be free!
Alas! and must I still complain -
  Deprived of liberty.

Oh, Heaven! and is there no relief
  This side the silent grave -
To soothe the pain to quell the grief
  And anguish of a slave?

Come Liberty, thou cheerful sound,
  Roll through my ravished ears!
Come, let my grief in joys be drowned,
  And drive away my fears.

Say unto foul oppression, Cease:
  Ye tyrants rage no more,
And let the joyful trump of peace,
  Now bid the vassal soar.

Soar on the pinions of that dove
  Which long has cooed for thee,
And breathed her notes from Afric's grove,
  The sound of Liberty.

Oh, Liberty! thou golden prize,
  So often sought by blood -
We crave thy sacred sun to rise,
  The gift of nature's God!

Bid Slavery hide her haggard face,
  And barbarism fly:
I scorn to see the sad disgrace
  In which enslaved I lie.

Dear Liberty! upon thy breast,
  I languish to respire;
And like the Swan unto her nest,
  I'd to thy smiles retire.

Oh, blest asylum heavenly balm!
  Unto thy boughs I flee -
And in thy shades the storm shall calm,
  With songs of Liberty!

To Eliza

Eliza, tell thy lover why
Or what induced thee to deceive me?
Fare thee well - away I fly -
I shun the lass who thus will grieve me.

Eliza, still thou art my song,
Although by force I may forsake thee;
Fare thee well, for I was wrong
To woo thee while another take thee.

Eliza, pause and think awhile -
Sweet lass! I shall forget thee never:
Fare thee well! although I smile,
I grieve to give thee up for ever.

Eliza, I shall think of thee -
My heart shall ever twine about thee;
Fare thee well but think of me,
Compell'd to live and die without thee.
   "Fare thee well! and if for ever,
Still for ever fare thee well!"

Love

Whilst tracing thy visage, I sink in emotion,
   For no other damsel so wond'rous I see;
Thy looks are so pleasing, thy charms so amazing,
   I think of no other, my true-love, but thee.

With heart-burning rapture I gaze on thy beauty,
   And fly like a bird to the boughs of a tree;
Thy looks are so pleasing, thy charms so amazing,
   I fancy no other, my true-love, but thee.

Thus oft in the valley I think, and I wonder
   Why cannot a maid with her lover agree?
Thy looks are so pleasing, thy charms so amazing,
   I pine for no other, my true-love, but thee.

I'd fly from thy frowns with a heart full of sorrow
   Return, pretty damsel, and smile thou on me;
By every endeavour, I'll try thee for ever,
   And languish until I am fancied by thee,

On The Death of an Infant

Blest Babe! it at length has withdrawn,
   The Seraphs have rocked it to sleep;
Away with an angelic smile it has gone,
   And left a sad parent to weep!

It soars from the ocean of pain,
   On breezes of precious perfume;
O be not discouraged when death is but gain
   The triumph of life from the tomb.

With pleasure I thought it my own,
   And smil'd on its infantile charms;
But some mystic bird, like an eagle, came down,
   And snatch'd it away from my arms.

Blest Babe, it ascends into Heaven,
   It mounts with delight at the call;
And flies to the bosom from whence it was given,
   The Parent and Patron of all.

The Slave's Complaint

Am I sadly cast aside,
On misfortune's rugged tide?
Will the world my pains deride
                For ever?

Must I dwell in Slavery's night,
And all pleasure take its flight,
Far beyond my feeble sight,
                For ever?

Worst of all, must Hope grow dim,
And withhold her cheering beam?
Rather let me sleep and dream
                For ever!

Something still my heart surveys,
Groping through this dreary maze;
Is it Hope] then burn and blaze
                For ever!

Leave me not a wretch confined,
Altogether lame and blind
Unto gross despair consigned,
                For ever!

Heaven! in whom can I confide?
Canst thou not for ail provide?
Condescend to be my guide
                    For ever:

And when this transient life shall end,
Oh, may some kind, eternal friend
Bid me from servitude ascend,
                    For ever!

On The Truth of the Saviour

E'en John the Baptist did not know
   Who Christ the Lord could be,
And bade his own disciples go,
   The strange event to see.

They said, Art thou the one of whom
   'Twas written long before?
Is there another still to come,
   Who will all things restore?

This is enough, without a name
   Go, tell him what is done;
Behold the feeble, weak and lame,
   With strength rise up and run.

This is enough - the blind now see,
   The dumb Hosannas sing;
Devils far from his presence flee,
   As shades from morning's wing.

See the distress'd, all bathed in tears,
   Prostrate before him fall;
Immanuel speaks, and Lazarus hears -
   The dead obeys his call.

This is enough - the fig-tree dies,
    And withers at his frown;
Nature her God must recognise,
    And drop her flowery crown.

At his command the fish increase,
    And loaves of barley swell -
Ye hungry eat, and hold your peace,
    And find a remnant still.

At his command the water blushed.
    And all was turned to wine,
And in redundance flowed afresh,
    And owned its God divine.

Behold the storms at his rebuke,
    All calm upon the sea -
How can we for another look,
    When none can work as he?

This is enough - it must be God,
    From whom the plagues are driven;
At whose command the mountains nod
    And all the Host of Heaven!

On Spring

Hail, thou auspicious vernal dawn!
Ye birds, proclaim the winter's gone,
    Ye warbling minstrels sing;
Pour forth your tribute as ye rise,
And thus salute the fragrant skies
    The pleasing smiles of Spring.

Coo sweetly, oh thou harmless Dove,
And bid thy mate no longer rove,
    In cold, hybernal vales;
Let music rise from every tongue,
Whilst winter flies before the song,
    Which floats on gentle gales.

Ye frozen streams dissolve and flow
Along the valley, sweet and slow;
    Divested fields be gay;
Ye drooping forests bloom on high,
And raise your branches to the sky,
    And thus your charms display.

Thou world of heat thou vital source,
The torpid insects feel thy force,
    Which all with life supplies;
Gardens and orchards richly bloom,

And send a gale of sweet perfume,
    To invite them as they rise.

Near where the crystal waters glide,
The male of birds escorts his bride,
    And twitters on the spray;
He mounts upon his active wing,
To hail the bounty of the Spring,
    The lavish pomp of May.

Inspiring month of youthful Love,
How oft we in the peaceful grove,
    Survey the flowery plume;
Or sit beneath the sylvan shade,
Where branches wave above the head,
    And smile on every bloom.

Exalted month, when thou art gone,
May Virtue then begin the dawn
    Of an eternal Spring"?
May raptures kindle on my tongue,
And start a new, eternal song,
    Which ne'er shall cease to ring!

On Summer

Esteville fire begins to burn;
   The auburn fields of harvest rise;
The torrid flames again return,
   And thunders roll along the skies.

Perspiring Cancer lifts his head,
   And roars terrific from on high;
Whose voice the timid creatures dread,
   From which they strive with awe to fly.

The night-hawk ventures from his cell,
   And starts his note in evening air;
He feels the heat his bosom swell,
   Which drives away the gloom of fear.

Thou noisy insect, start thy drum;
   Rise lamp-like bugs to light the train;
And bid sweet Philomela come,
   And sound in front the nightly strain.

The bee begins her ceaseless hum,
   And doth with sweet exertions rise;
And with delight she stores her comb,
   And well her rising stock supplies.

Let sportive children well beware,
   While sprightly frisking o'er the green;
And carefully avoid the snare,
   Which lurks beneath the smiling scene.

The mistress bird assumes her nest,
   And broods in silence on the tree,
Her note to cease, her wings at rest,
   She patient waits her young to see.

The farmer hastens from the heat;
   The weary plough-horse droops his head;
The cattle all at noon retreat,
   And ruminate beneath the shade.

The burdened ox with dauntless rage,
   Flies heedless to the liquid flood,
From which he quaffs, devoid of guage,
   Regardless of his driver's rod.

Pomaceous orchards now expand
   Their laden branches o'er the lea
And with their bounty fill the land,
   While plenty smiles on every tree.

On fertile borders, near the stream,
   Now gaze with pleasure and delight;
See loaded vines with melons teem -
   'Tis paradise to human sight.

With rapture view the smiling fields,
   Adorn the mountain and the plain,
Each, on the eve of Autumn, yields
   A large supply of golden grain.

On Winter

When smiling Summer's charms are past.
   The voice of music dies;
Then Winter pours his chilling blast
   From rough inclement skies.

The pensive dove shuts up her throat,
   The larks forbear to soar,
Or raise one sweet, delightful note,
   Which charm'd the ear before.

The screech-owl peals her shivering tone
   Upon the brink of night;
As some sequestered child unknown,
   Which feared to come in sight.

The cattle all desert the field,
   And eager seek the glades
Of naked trees, which once did yield
   Their sweet and pleasant shades.

The humming insects all are still,
   The beetles rise no more,
The constant tinkling of the bell,
   Along the heath is o'er.

Stern Boreas hurls each piercing gale
   With snow-clad wings along,
Discharging volleys mixed with hail
   Which chill the breeze of song.

Lo, all the Southern windows close,
   Whence spicy breezes roll;
The herbage sinks in sad repose,
   And Winter sweeps the whole.

Thus after youth old age comes on,
   And brings the frost of time.
And e'er our vigour has withdrawn,
   We shed the rose of prime.

Alas! how quick it is the case,
   The scion youth is grown -
How soon it runs its morning race.
   And beauty's sun goes down.

The Autumn of declining years
   Must blanch the father's head,
Encumbered with a load of cares,
   When youthful charms have fled.

Heavenly Love

Eternal spring of boundless grace,
    It lifts the soul above,
Where God the Son unveils his face,
    And shows that Heaven is love.

Love that revolves through endless years
    Love that can never pall;
Love which excludes the gloom of fears,
    Love to whom God is all!

Love which can ransom every slave,
    And set the pris'ner free;
Gild the dark horrors of the grave,
    And still the raging sea.

Let but the partial smile of Heaven
    Upon the bosom play,
The mystic sound of sins forgiven,
    Can waft the soul away.

The pilgrim's spirits show this love,
    They often soar on high;
Languish from this dim earth to move.
    And leave the flesh to die.

Sing, oh my soul, rise up and run,
    And leave this clay behind;
Wing thy swift flight beyond the sun,
    Nor dwell in tents confined.

On The Death of Rebecca

Thou delicate blossom! thy short race is ended,
   Thou sample of virtue and prize of the brave!
No more are thy beauties by mortals attended, .
   They now are but food for the worms and the grave.

Thou art gone to the tomb, whence there's no returning,
   And left us behind in a vale of suspense;
In vain to the dust do we follow thee mourning,
   The same doleful trump will soon call us all hence.

I view thee now launched on eternity's ocean,
   Thy soul how it smiles as it floats on the wave;
It smiles as if filled with the softest emotion,
   But looks not behind on the frowns of the grave.

The messenger came from afar to relieve thee -
   In this lonesome valley no more shalt thou roam;
Bright seraphs now stand on the banks to receive thee,
   And cry, "Happy stranger, thou art welcome at home."

Thou art gone to a feast, while thy friends are bewailing,
   Oh, death is a song to the poor ransom'd slave;
Away with bright visions the spirit goes sailing,
   And leaves the frail body to rest in the grave.

Rebecca is free from the pains of oppression,
    No friends could prevail with her longer to stay;
She smiles on the fields of eternal fruition,
    Whilst death like a bridegroom attends her away.

She is gone in the whirlwind - ye seraphs attend her,
    Through Jordan's cold torrent her mantle may lave;
She soars in the chariot, and earth falls beneath her,
    Resign'd in a shroud to a peaceable grave.

On Death

Deceitful worm, that undermines the clay,
Which slyly steals the thoughtless soul away,
Pervading neighborhoods with sad surprise,
Like sudden storms of wind and thunder rise.

The sounding death-watch lurks within the wall,
Away some unsuspecting soul to call;
The pendant willow droops her waving head,
And sighing zephyrs whisper of the dead.

Methinks I hear the doleful midnight knell -
Some parting spirit bids the world farewell;
The taper burns as conscious of distress,
And seems to show the living numberless.

Must a lov'd daughter from her father part,
And grieve for one who lies so near her heart?
And must she for the fatal loss bemoan,
Or faint to hear his last departing groan.

Methinks I see him speechless gaze awhile,
And on her drop his last paternal smile;
With gushing tears closing his humid eyes,
The last pulse beats, and in her arms he dies.

With pallid cheeks she lingers round his bier,
And heaves a farewell sigh with every tear;
With sorrow she consigns him to the dust,
And silent owns the fatal sentence just.

Still her sequestered mother seems to weep,
And spurns the balm which constitutes her sleep;
Her plaintive murmurs float upon the gale,
And almost make the stubborn rocks bewail.

O what is like the awful breach of death,
Whose fatal stroke invades the creature's breath!
It bids the voice of desolation roll,
And strikes the deepest awe within the bravest soul.

On The Evening and Morning

When Evening bids the Sun to rest retire,
Unwearied Ether sets her lamps on fire;
Lit by one torch, each is supplied in turn,
Till all the candles in the concave burn.

The night-hawk now, with his nocturnal tone,
Wakes up, and all the Owls begin to moan,
Or heave from dreary vales their dismal song,
Whilst in the air the meteors play along.

At length the silver queen begins to rise,
And spread her glowing mantle in the skies,
And from the smiling chambers of the east,
Invites the eye to her resplendent feast.

What joy is this unto the rustic swain,
Who from the mount surveys the moon-lit plain;
Who with the spirit of a dauntless *Pan*
Controls his fleecy train and leads the van;

Or pensive, muses on the water's side,
Which purling doth thro' green meanders glide,
With watchful care he broods his heart away
'Till night is swallowed in the flood of day.

The meteors cease to play, that mov'd so fleet
And spectres from the murky groves retreat,
The prowling wolf withdraws, which howl'd so bold
And bleating flocks may venture from the fold.

The night-hawk's din deserts the shepherd's ear,
Succeeded by the huntsman's trumpet clear,
O come Diana, start the morning chase
Thou ancient goddess of the hunting race.

Aurora's smiles adorn the mountain's brow,
The peasant hums delighted at his plough,
And lo, the dairy maid salutes her bounteous cow.

On The Poetic Muse

Far, far above this world I soar,
   And almost nature lose,
Aerial regions to explore,
   With this ambitious Muse,

My towering thoughts with pinions rise,
   Upon the gales of song,
Which waft me through the mental skies,
   With music on my tongue.

My Muse is all on mystic fire,
   Which kindles in my breast;
To scenes remote she doth aspire,
   As never yet exprest.

Wrapt in the dust she scorns to lie,
   Call'd by new charms away;
Nor will she e'er refuse to try
   Such wonders to survey.

Such is the quiet, bliss of soul,
   When in some calm retreat,
Where pensive thoughts like streamlets roll,
   And render silence sweet;

And when the vain tumultuous crowd
  Shakes comfort from my mind,
My muse ascends above the cloud
  And leaves the noise behind.

With vivid flight she mounts on high
  Above the dusky maze,
And with a perspicacious eye
  Doth far 'bove nature gaze.

Consequences of Happy Marriages

Hail happy pair, from whom such raptures rise,
On whom I gaze with pleasure and surprise;
From thy bright rays the gloom of strife is driven,
For all the smiles of mutual love are Heaven.

Thrice happy pair! no earthly joys excel
Thy peaceful state; there constant pleasures dwell,
Which cheer the mind and elevate the soul,
Whilst discord sinks beneath their soft control.

The blaze of zeal extends from breast to breast,
While Heaven supplies each innocent request;
And lo! what fond regard their smiles reveal,
Attractive as the magnet to the steel.

Their peaceful life is all content and ease,
They with delight each other strive to please;
Each other's charms, *they* only can admire,
Whose bosoms burn with pure connubial fire.

Th' indelible vestige of unblemished love,
Must hence a guide to generations prove:
Though virtuous partners moulder in the tomb,
Their light may shine on ages yet to come.

With grateful tears their well-spent day shall close,
When death, like evening, calls them to repose;
Then mystic smiles may break from deep disguise,
Like Vesper's torch transpiring in the skies.

Like constellations still their works may shine,
In virtue's unextinguished blaze divine;
Happy are they whose race shall end the same -
Sweeter than odours is a virtuous name.

Such is the transcript of unfading grace,
Reflecting lustre on a future race,
The virtuous on this line delight to tread,
And magnify the honors of the dead -

Who like a Phoenix did not burn in vain,
Incinerated to revive again;
From whose exalted urn young love shall rise,
Exulting from a funeral sacrifice.

Lines

On hearing of the intention of a gentleman to purchase the Poet's freedom.

When on life's ocean first I spread my sail,
I then implored a mild auspicious gale;
And from the slippery strand I took my flight,
And sought the peaceful haven of delight.

Tyrannic storms arose upon my soul,
And dreadful did their mad'ning thunders roll;
The pensive muse was shaken from her sphere,
And hope, it vanish'd in the clouds of fear.

At length a golden sun broke through the gloom,
And from his smiles arose a sweet perfume -
A calm ensued, and birds began to sing,
And lo! the sacred muse resumed her wing.

With frantic joy she chaunted as she flew,
And kiss'd the clement hand that bore her through;
Her envious foes did from her sight retreat,
Or prostrate fall beneath her burning feet.

'Twas like a proselyte, allied to Heaven -
Or rising spirits' boast of sins forgiven,
Whose shout dissolves the adamant away,

"Whose melting voice the stubborn rocks obey.

'Twas like the salutation of the dove,
Borne on the zephyr through some lonesome grove,
When Spring returns, and Winter's chill is past,
And vegetation smiles above the blast.

"Twas like the evening of a nuptial pair,
When love pervades the hour of sad despair -
'Twas like fair Helen's sweet return to Troy,
When every Grecian bosom swell'd with joy.

The silent harp which on the osiers hung,
Was then attuned, and manumission sung:
Away by hope the clouds of fear were driven,
And music breathed my gratitude to Heaven.

Hard was the race to reach the distant goal,
The needle oft was shaken from the pole;
In such distress who could forbear to weep?
Toss'd by the headlong billows of the deep!

The tantalizing beams which shone so plain,
Which turned my former pleasures into pain -
Which falsely promised all the joys of fame,
Gave way, and to a more substantial flame.

Some philanthropic souls as from afar,
With pity strove to break the slavish bar;

To whom my floods of gratitude shall roll,
And yield with pleasure to their soft control.

And sure of Providence this work begun -
He shod my feet this rugged race to run;
And in despite of all the swelling tide,
Along the dismal path will prove my guide.

Thus on the dusky verge of deep despair,
Eternal Providence was with me there;
When pleasure seemed to fade on life's gay dawn,
And the last beam of hope was almost gone.

To The Gad-Fly

Majestic insect! from thy royal hum,
The flies retreat, or starve before they'll come;
The obedient plough-horse may, devoid of fear,
Perform his task with joy, when thou art near.

As at the Lion's dread alarming roar,
The inferior beasts will never wander more,
Lest unawares he should be seized away,
And to the prowling monster fall a prey.

With silent pleasure often do I trace
The fly upon the wing, with rapid pace,
The fugitive proclaims upon the wind,
The death-bound sheriff is not far behind.

Ye thirsty flies beware, nor dare approach,
Nor on the toiling animal encroach;
Be vigilant, before yon buzz too late,
The victim of a melancholy fate.

Such seems the caution of the once chased fly,
Whilst to the horse she dare not venture nigh;
This useful Gad-Fly traversing the field,
With care the lab'ring animal to shield.

Such is the eye of Providential care.
Along the path of life forever there;
Whose guardian hand by day doth mortals keep
And gently lays them down at night to sleep.

Immortal Guard, shall I thy pleasures grieve
Like Noah's dove, wilt thou the creature leave;
No never, never, whilst on earth I stay,
And after death, then fly with me away.

The Loss of Female Character

See that fallen Princess! her splendor is gone -
The pomp of her morning is over;
Her day-star of pleasure refuses to dawn,
She wanders a nocturnal rover,

Alas! she resembles Jerusalem's fall,
The fate of that wonderful city;
When grief with astonishment rung from the wall,
Instead of the heart cheering ditty.

When music was silent, no more to be rung,
When Sion wept over her daughter;
On grief's drooping willow their harps they were hung,
When pendent o'er Babylon's water.

She looks like some Star that has fall'n from her sphere,
No more by her cluster surrounded;
Her comrades of pleasure refuse her to cheer,
And leave her dethron'd and confounded.

She looks like some Queen who has boasted in vain,
Whose diamond refuses to glitter;
Deserted by those who once bow'd in her train,
Whose flight to her soul must be bitter.

She looks like the twilight, her sun sunk away,
He sets; but to rise again never!
Like the Eve, with a blush bids farewell to the day,
And darkness conceals her forever.